The Persuasive Negotiator

Proven Techniques for Getting What You Want

Lawrence Leonard White

Table of Contents

Negotiation in the classic diplomatic sense assumes parties more anxious to agree than to disagree.

— Dean Acheson

Chapter 1. Introduction

The world of negotiation can often feel like uncharted territory, full of obstacles and pitfalls. But what if you had a road map? A guide to navigate you expertly through those tricky discussions, to emerge, not only unscathed, but triumphant. Our Special Report, "The Persuasive Negotiator: Proven Techniques for Getting What You Want", is exactly that guide! Bursting with proven strategies and effective approaches, this report will arm you with the tools needed to transform you into a master negotiator. It's time to uncover the secrets of persuasive negotiation and learn how to effortlessly swerve around roadblocks, navigate detours, and reach your desired destination every time. If success is your ultimate goal, acquire this Special Report today — your future self will thank you!

Chapter 2. Introduction to Negotiation: The Art of Persuasion

Negotiation is a fundamental part of our daily life, infiltrating every interaction, whether personal or professional. Be it negotiating an annual raise with your boss, discussing chores with your kids, or navigating a high-stakes business deal, negotiation is the art form that underpins it all. This is the core concept upon which we'll build in this initial exploration of negotiation and persuasion.

2.1. Understanding Negotiation

Negotiation is a process that comes into play in scenarios where multiple parties are involved, each with differing desires and goals, striving to reach a common ground. It is the activity of comparison and contrast, a dance between demands and offers, towards a shared outcome satisfactory for all.

At its core, every negotiation revolves around five essential elements: Interests, preferences, legitimacy, communication, and relationship. Each of these acts as a pillar for successful negotiation: Alone they offer minor leverage, but together, they build a comprehensive negotiation strategy.

As we delve deeper into each of these elements, you'll be equipped with a roadmap to unlock your inner negotiator, and the approach to leverage each element to maximize your advantage.

2.2. Fundamental Elements of Negotiation

Interests refer to the foundation upon which negotiation is built. This is the 'why' that drives both parties to the table. It could be tangible, such as a salary increment, or intangible, like reputation improvement. The more comprehensively you understand your interests, the better your chance at negotiation success.

Preferences outline the options or possible outcomes you find acceptable in a negotiation scenario. Aligning preferences amongst conflicting parties is a key challenge in negotiation but also provides the opportunity for creative solutions.

Legitimacy accounts for the fairness, equity, and balance of the negotiation. It's about harnessing the power of norms, standards, and even external validations to bring credibility to your stance.

Communication is pivotal to express interests, preferences, and legitimacy effectively. It involves both verbal and non-verbal cues, fostering a shared understanding, and purposefully directing the negotiation.

Relationship, the last key aspect of negotiation, underlines the importance of the human connection. It emphasizes long-term collaboration over momentary wins, promoting trust, respect, and flexibility as paramount to sustained negotiation success.

2.3. Persuasion: The Magic Ingredient

Once the foundational elements of negotiation are understood, it's time to introduce the magic ingredient – persuasion. It is indeed the secret sauce that adds flavor to your negotiation, pulling your interests firmly towards the favorable end of the spectrum. Excelling in persuasion can mean the difference between seizing life-changing opportunities and missing out on them entirely. The right persuasive techniques, when wielded with precision and sincerity, can open the doors to endless possibilities.

Persuasive negotiation begins with understanding the audience, deciphering their goals and motivations, getting ahead of their objections, and addressing them proactively. The ability to artfully persuade can turn potential stumbling blocks into stepping stones, giving you an edge in your negotiation journey. While nudging the other party towards your point of view, always bear in mind the principle of mutual respect and aim for a win-win scenario.

Moreover, persuasion doesn't cease at the negotiation table; it extends to building consensus among stakeholders, managing perceptions, and nurturing relationships for the long haul. By demonstrating reliable credibility, emotional intelligence, and strategic agility, you can become a formidable persuader.

2.4. Wrapping Up

This introduction to negotiation and persuasion has barely scratched the surface of this rich and complex subject. As we progress through the subsequent chapters of this book, each element will be dissected, analyzed, and explored in greater depth, setting the stage for a transformative learning journey. Prepare to venture into the fascinating universe of negotiation, where words become tools, actions turn into influence, and relationships shape as the key to unlocking opportunities. Happy negotiating!

Chapter 3. Understanding Your Negotiation Style

Every negotiation journey begins with a deep understanding of one's self. Just as a compass points north, your negotiation compass—at its core—is your negotiation style. Recognizing your prevailing style and how it impacts your engagements with others is the first step along the path to becoming a more effective and persuasive negotiator.

3.1. Recognizing the Five Negotiation Styles

Think of your negotiation style as a filter through which you perceive, process, and react in negotiation situations. There are generally five recognized negotiation styles: Competing, Collaborating, Compromising, Avoiding, and Accommodating.

The Competing style, as the name suggests, views negotiation as a zero-sum game; one in which there is a clear winner and a clear loser. If you fall into this category, you are likely to be assertive, possess high levels of self-esteem, and prioritize achieving your objectives over preserving relationships.

The Collaborating style, on the other hand, is a partnership approach to negotiation where all parties work together to reach a solution that satisfies everyone's needs. This style requires high emotional intelligence, excellent communication skills, and the ability to empathize with other team members.

The Compromising style is essentially a balancing act. If you lean towards this style, you aim for a give-and-take approach in order to quickly reach a mutually agreeable solution—all the while preserving relationships and ensuring fairness.

Avoiders tend to steer clear of conflicts and confrontations. If your style aligns with Avoiding, you're likely to defer, withdraw, or sidestep negotiation, often leaving issues unresolved.

Lastly, Accommodating individuals are those who prioritize relationship preservation above all else. If this is your style, you are likely to make concessions, even at your own disadvantage, just to keep the peace and maintain goodwill.

3.2. Conducting a Self-Assessment

Understanding your style is a process of introspection and self-evaluation. Observation and reflection on past negotiations can be a great starting point. Look for patterns in your responses to conflict and instances where you've had to assert your interests or make concessions. Self-assessment tools are another useful resource. Instruments such as the Thomas-Kilmann Conflict Mode Instrument (TKI) can provide insights into your prevailing style.

3.3. Balancing Your Negotiation Style

While there may be one style you feel most comfortable with, becoming a persuasive negotiator requires the ability to adapt your style based on the situation, the people involved, and the specific objectives at hand. Balancing your style means understanding when, how, and why to employ different negotiation techniques.

For instance, during a high-stakes negotiation where the relationship with the other party is not a priority, it could be beneficial to adopt a Competing style. However, in situations where preserving the relationship is important, Collaborating or Accommodating may be the better choice.

3.4. Cultivating an Adaptive Negotiation Style

Adapting your negotiation style requires self-awareness and flexibility. Recognize your biases and tendencies, but don't be ruled by them. Expand your negotiation toolkit by learning and practicing skills associated with other styles.

Role-playing exercises can offer a practical way to gain experience with different approaches. By stepping into the shoes of a different style, we can truly understand its strengths and weaknesses, and learn how to use it effectively in real negotiations.

Developing an adaptive style is a journey, not a destination. It involves continuous learning, and the willingness to step out of your comfort zone. But if you commit to this journey, you'll find that it broadens your horizons, enhances your growth, and ultimately, sharpens your edge as a negotiator.

3.5. The Impact of Personal Bias and Cognitive Distortions

Personal biases and cognitive distortions can also have a significant impact on your negotiation style. These automated, unconscious brain functions can lead to irrational decisions and skewed perceptions during a negotiation. Understanding your cognitive biases and how these affect your negotiation style will further enhance your ability to adapt and negotiate effectively.

With time and introspection, you'll not only better understand your negotiation style and its impact, but also how to harness, refine, and adapt it based on the situation at hand. With this mastery, you are then well-positioned to steer any negotiation towards your desired outcome, all while maintaining productive relationships.

Chapter 4. The Power of Active Listening in Negotiations

To fully comprehend the far-reaching influence of active listening in negotiations, we must first establish an in-depth understanding of the basic elements that construct this integral component of conversation. Listening, in its simplest form, is fundamentally a cognitive process of decoding auditory input. Yet, in the realm of human interactions, merely deciphering the sounds emanating from utterances falls woefully short of truly understanding the meanings, nuances, and subtleties imbued within them.

4.1. The Essence of Active Listening

Active listening transcends the passive absorption of words. It's an engaged process, wherein the listener strives to comprehend, retain, and respond to the speaker's messages. This heightened form of listening encapsulates multiple facets — from the non-verbal to the verbal, the overt to the hidden. With its primary aim of demonstrating respect and understanding towards the speaker, active listening promotes healthy dialogue, fosters positive relationships and, ultimately, drives successful negotiations.

4.2. Active Listening: A Multi-Dimensional Process

Unpacking active listening reveals it to be a multi-dimensional process, divided into several key components: receiving, understanding, remembering, evaluating, and responding, each transcending the prior level of communication engagement.

Receiving is the initial step, a foundational level that involves capturing and acknowledging the delivery of a message. This involves noticing both the verbal content and the non-verbal cues that accompany it. **Understanding** takes the process one step further; the listener must process the received content and interpret its intended meanings. **Remembering** is about the storage and mental cataloguing of information received and understood. **Evaluation** employs critical thinking skills, as the listener analyzes and judges the content comprehended and memory-stored. Finally, **responding** provides feedback to the speaker, confirming that their message is being listened to proactively.

4.3. Active Listening in Negotiations

In the landscape of negotiation, active listening wields great influence. It serves as an indispensable tool in any negotiator's skillset, playing a dual role as both charitable trust-building mechanism and tactical information acquiring method. Listeners who truly engage with their conversation partner's discourse not only gain a deeper understanding of their needs, interests, and concerns, but they are also more apt to identify potential pain points and opportunities that can be tactically used to their advantage later in the negotiation.

4.4. Techniques for Active Listening in Negotiations

To leap from the realm of theory to the tangible dimension of practice, it is pertinent for the would-be master negotiator to embrace certain techniques that aid active listening. These principles include - maintaining eye contact, demonstrating non-verbal engagement, offering verbal affirmations, refraining from interrupting, summarizing crucial points, asking open-ended questions, and providing accurate feedback.

Maintaining eye contact signals interest and respect to the speaker, thereby promoting trust. **Demonstrating non-verbal engagement** can be as simple as nodding, leaning forward, or mirroring the speaker's gestures. **Offering verbal affirmations**, using simple phrases like "I see" or "I understand", indicates that the listener is present and tuned into the speaker's narrative. **Refraining from interrupting** gives the speaker the time and space they need to fully express their thoughts. **Summarizing crucial points** is a method of restating or paraphrasing the speaker's key arguments or ideas, validating their message and demonstrating comprehension. **Asking open-ended questions** godfathers deeper conversation, opening avenues for the speaker to explore their thoughts in greater detail. Finally, **providing accurate feedback** helps to clarify any misconceptions and encourage further meaningful dialogue.

4.5. Challenges and Solutions

Of course, the pursuit of active listening is not without challenges. Distractions, assumptions, and emotional responses represent barriers that impair effective active listening. However, the key to overcoming these obstacles lies in self-awareness, self-management, and a genuine curiosity about the speaker's perspective.

Ultimately, the power of active listening in negotiations pierces through the walls of misunderstanding to illuminate a path of connection and possibility. It's an ever-present compass, guiding negotiators through thickets of contention and conflict towards a destination of agreement and mutual benefit. Imbued with understanding, patience, and empathy, the active listener is poised to unlock the true potential of negotiations, transforming objections into opportunities, disputes into agreements, and simple conversations into powerful negotiations. Only by channeling the art of active listening can one truly attain the status of a persuasive, effective negotiator.

Chapter 5. Decoding Non-Verbal Communication

The journey to transformational negotiation skills is paved with a variety of important strategies, and one critical facet of this intricate mosaic is non-verbal communication. Herein lies the power to convey unspoken agreement, disagreement, confusion, understanding, and myriad other reactions, emotions, and states of mind. More often than not, it's the silent dialogue we carry on through our body language, facial expressions, eye contact, and overall demeanor that speaks louder than words. They lay the fertile grounds for interpretation, setting the tone for our negotiations.

5.1. Unveiling the Language of the Body

Much like how a coded message requires a specific decryption key, understanding non-verbal cues requires the adept decryption skills of a seasoned negotiator. This non-verbal language adds a layer of depth to our communication, often revealing more than spoken words.

Eye contact, an integral part of non-verbal communication, can signal attentiveness and respect or, when averted, might showcase uneasiness or evasion. A firm and confident posture radiates power and conviction, while slouching or drawing inward could be perceived as insecure or defensive. Our hand gestures can emphasize, illustrate, or negate the words we've spoken.

It's crucial to observe these non-verbal cues in our counterparts to decipher their feelings or thoughts that might remain unspoken. For instance, if the other party seems to retreat or becomes stiff and guarded physically, it may indicate discomfort or an impending objection, serving as a cue for you to adjust your approach.

5.2. The Echoes of Facial Expressions

Researchers estimate that we can produce around 7,000 facial expressions, a vast expanse of non-verbal signals. They can be subtle, fleeting, or dramatic, making the face a powerful canvas for projecting emotions – excitement, worry, disagreement, uncertainty, openness, and more.

An intently focused look may show genuine interest or curiosity, while softening that intensity might indicate confusion or polite disagreement. A spontaneous smile communicates warmth and approachability, but when these smiles become infrequent or too brief, they might betray a lack of sincerity. Awareness of such nuances can provide additional layers to our understanding of the negotiation process.

5.3. Navigating the Spectrum of Personal Space

Personal space, although silent, can speak volumes about one's feelings of comfort or discomfort. Penetrating someone's personal space might indicate assertiveness, but it can also be seen as intrusive and potentially cause discomfort, thereby negatively affecting the negotiation outcomes.

Careful attention to these spatial cues can give you an upper hand in determining the next best course of action. If an individual appears to shrink away or builds barriers through gestures like crossing their arms, it might serve as a signal to take a step back, both physically and figuratively.

5.4. The Unspoken Discourse of Touch

In the context of negotiations, touch can span the gamut from reassuring to aggressive. A firm handshake at the beginning of a meeting instills an immediate sense of trust and respect. Conversely, an overly firm handshake can be perceived as excessively assertive or dominant.

Endeavor to understand the meaning of touch in different cultures, as the acceptability and interpretation of touch can vary widely. What is reassuring in one culture might be seen as invasive or disrespectful in another.

5.5. Harnessing the Voice's Silent Power

While the spoken word carries the message's content, the voice's tone, pitch, and speed can convey additional non-verbal cues. A fast-paced talker might be perceived as nervous or eager, while a slow, steady pace suggests confidence and control. Pitch can also express emotions – higher when excited or stressed and lower when calm or serious.

Studying and adapting to your counterpart's vocal cues could help to influence the rhythm and flow of conversation, fostering a conducive environment for negotiation.

Mastering the art of decoding non-verbal communication is a dynamic and demanding process, requiring attentive observation, accurate interpretation, and responsive adaptation. By effectively employing these skills, negotiators can navigate past surface-level words, tap into the unstated emotions, intentions, and reactions, and steer the discussion towards a mutually beneficial outcome.

Remember, in negotiations, nothing is trivial, every gesture, every silence, every nuance counts. Learn to listen with your eyes, your intuition, and your mind open, arming you with an array of intelligence about your counterpart, ensuring your path towards becoming a persuasive negotiator.

Chapter 6. Planning and Preparing: The Key to Successful Negotiations

In the grand orchestra of negotiation, planning and preparation are akin to the meticulous tuning up of the instruments before the concert begins. The process sets the tone and provides the readiness for the ensuing performance. Certainly, as a dedicated negotiator aiming to strike a harmonious chord, deep-dive planning and preparation is a prerequisite.

6.1. Understanding the Importance of Preparation in Negotiation

Preparation in negotiation is similar to the blueprint for an architect. It helps to create a sense of control, because it enables you to gauge and predict your counterpart's potential reactions and responses. But beyond providing this sense of control, preparation paves the way for creativity, facilitating the development of innovative solutions and unlocking value from impasses.

Preparation aids in defining the shape and trajectory of the negotiation process. It allows you to frame the negotiation in a way that benefits your interests, while still being considerate of the other side's concerns.

6.2. The Roles of Planning and Preparation

In successful negotiations, planning and preparation assume various pivotal roles. These roles fuse to create a robust negotiation strategy that is adaptable, proactive, and efficient.

1. **Defining Objectives and Goals:** A significant role of planning is to define the ultimate objectives and immediate goals of the negotiation. These outcomes should be realistic, specific, and adaptable given the dynamic nature of negotiation.

2. **Identifying Key Issues:** Taking the time to analyze the negotiation landscape will help you identify the key issues at stake.

3. **Researching the Counterpart:** Understand who you will be negotiating with. Grasp their objectives, negotiation style, and potential strategies.

4. **Preparing a Strategy:** Outlining a general strategy acts as the negotiation compass, guiding you through uncertain terrains.

5. **Practising the Negotiation:** Practising your negotiation helps you anticipate probable approaches and visualise the negotiation trajectory.

6.3. The Process of In-depth Planning and Preparation

The process of planning and preparing for a negotiation is a thorough one, composed of several integral steps meant to ensure the utmost readiness for your negotiation. Dedicate considerable time and effort to each of these significant steps.

1. **Defining Your Strategic Objectives:** To start with, you have to be clear on what you want to achieve from the negotiation. Clear objectives serve as the guiding light of your negotiation journey. They provide both direction and parameters, increasing your chances of securing a beneficial outcome. Always ensure that these objectives are realistic, specific, measurable, attainable, relevant, and time-bound (SMART).

2. **Researching Your Counterpart:** This step requires your careful attention. Understand the negotiating parties, their interests, constraints, needs, and preferred negotiation style. Gathering this information will enable you to fashion your strategies and tactics, adding an element of predictability to the negotiation process.

3. **Identifying the Key Issues:** What are the core issues in dispute? What are the obstacles hampering agreement? Extracting key issues helps in creating an issue-based agenda, which can guide the negotiation process and prevent unnecessary deviations.

4. **Creating a Negotiation Plan:** With your objectives, knowledge of the other party, and key issues at hand, it's time to frame a negotiation plan. This plan will serve as your high-level guide, containing a list of issues to be addressed, an ordered sequence for their discussion, and ideal and fallback positions for each issue.

5. **Practising the Negotiation:** Mock negotiations help you fine-tune your strategies, develop plausible responses to potential arguments, and improve your delivery. Regular practice also develops reflexes and enhances instinctive decision-making skills.

6.4. The Art of Adaptive Planning

Regardless of how thorough your planning and preparation, negotiation is not a predictable procedure. It's analogous to sailing on a winding river, where unexpected turns, rapids, and blockages are par for the course.

As such, planning shouldn't be a rigid procedure with concrete steps. Instead, it should employ adaptive planning. This involves creating a plan with options that can be dynamically adapted or changed according to the situation.

In the end, the strongest negotiators aren't just those who plan well, but those who balance meticulous planning with skillful improvisation, responding to the vicissitudes of the negotiation process with dexterity and confidence. And for that, thorough planning and preparation are indispensable. Through this chapter, we aim to stress on the importance of preparing and planning for a negotiation, and to guide you on the detailed steps to do so.

Chapter 7. Mastering the Art of Questioning

The capacity to ask the right question at the right time is a pivotal aspect of negotiation — it is pivotal, in fact, not just to negotiation but to all forms of communication. The skill of crafting effective and timely questions gives you an advantage by enabling you to control the narrative, probing underlying issues, and exposing potential opportunities. By offering insights into intentions, motives, needs, and emotions, questions can uncover key information that may have been left untold. The mastery of this art can be seen analogous to that of the seasoned fisherman, who knows the best bait to use, how to cast the line, and when to reel in the catch. Let's dive deep into the ocean of crafting and posing thoughtful questions which will lay the foundation for becoming a persuasive negotiator.

7.1. Knowing the Different Types of Questions

To begin, it is essential to understand the different kinds of questions at our disposal. The two primary types of questions you can employ in any conversation, including in your negotiations, are open-ended questions and close-ended questions.

Open-ended questions invite a full, meaningful answer. Their subjective nature encourages expansive responses, promotes conversation, and fosters a sense of equality and partnership. They offer the other party a chance to expand upon their thoughts, feelings, and views. Using open-ended questions demonstrates your genuine interest in their perceptions. Examples include, "How do you feel about the terms of the contract?" or "Can you explain more about your reservations?"

On the other hand, close-ended questions limit the response to a single word, like "yes" or "no" or a short phrase, thereby constraining the response options. Despite their restrictive nature, they come handy when you need concise, factual information, or to make the conversation more focussed and specific. For example, "Are you the final decision-maker regarding this deal?" or "Does your company have the resources to deliver what it promised?"

Both types of questions are valuable tools in different situations, and a keen negotiator knows when and how to use each effectively.

7.2. Asking Probing Questions

Probing questions are valuable tools in every negotiator's arsenal to delve deeper to uncover concealed issues, unravel complexities, and isolate another party's interests. Such questions help to reveal latent needs and anxieties, thus paving the way to breaking deadlock situations and fostering a collaborative ambiance. Examples include: "Why do you think this strategy works best?" or "What, in your opinion, are the challenges we might face, and how can we overcome them?"

These questions help fight the impulse to assume, and instead, promote a culture of exploring and discovering. This practice minimizes the risk of misunderstanding and misinformation and potentially opens up new paths for a mutually beneficial solution.

7.3. The Power of Tactical Questions

Tactical questions can be employed in a negotiation to ensure the other party considers your viewpoint. While these queries require more thoughtful construction, they can be extremely helpful to steer the conversation towards your preferred outcome. By leading through questions, you subtly impress upon the other party to see things as you do - which in turn promotes an environment where mutual gains are more likely to be identified. For example, posing a question such as, "If we could find a way to meet your delivery dates while maintaining our quality, would you be open to rethinking the contract terms?" marries your needs with their requirements, subtly influencing their perspective towards your proposition.

7.4. Reflective and Clarifying Questions

Reflective questions work towards demonstrating your understanding and empathy towards the other party. It involves rephrasing or parroting back what the other party has said, as a question, to confirm that you correctly understand their viewpoint. For instance, "So, just to clarify, you're concerned about the delivery timelines being too tight, correct?" This kind of question fosters mutual understanding, which is crucial to successful negotiation.

In similar lines, clarifying questions aim to ensure that you have indeed understood the other party's points. These questions are used to confirm, clarify, or more fully explore the assertions or claims of the other party, such as, "When you say 'better terms,' can you be more explicit about what you're looking for?"

7.5. Counterfactual Questions

Counterfactual questions involve asking about hypothetical scenarios which diverge from reality. These could range from exploring alternative pasts to envisioning different future outcomes. For example, "Had we agreed to those conditions initially, would we be facing these issues?" or "If we keep the current pace, will we be able to complete the project as planned?" It allows the parties involved in the negotiation to think creatively, consider alternative options, and anticipate potential challenges and opportunities.

In conclusion, the art of questioning is a robust tool, empowering you with more control over the negotiation process and the potential outcomes. Mastering it not only helps to uncover valuable information, but also aids in building relationships and finding creative solutions to issues, thereby leading to more successful negotiation outcomes. The strength of your question-asking ability often directly dictates the efficacy of your negotiations. So, pay due consideration to harnessing this powerful skill – your success as a negotiator depends on it.

Chapter 8. Influence, Power, and Leverage: Maximizing Your Advantage

Before delving into the intricacies of influence, power, and leverage in negotiation, it is crucial to establish their individual definitions. Influence refers to the capacity to affect others' decisions or actions subtly, power constitutes the ability to shape outcomes more unilaterally and often overtly, and leverage is the strategic advantage or strength one party holds over another in a negotiation process.

8.1. The Dynamics of Influence in Negotiation

Influence is the most subtle of the three concepts. Applying influence effectively during negotiation requires an understanding of human behavior and effective interpersonal communication. Influence operates indirectly, encouraging the other party to see things from your point of view without resorting to coercion or pressure.

One of the proven techniques for exerting influence in negotiations is the principle of reciprocity, which is deeply ingrained in human behavior. This principle entails giving something — like a concession, a favor, or useful information — to the other party in the hopes that they will feel obliged to reciprocate in kind. For example, by sharing some valuable information with your negotiating counterpart, you might create an unspoken expectation for them to share some crucial information in return.

Another successful technique of influence is the principle of consistency. People generally strive for consistency in their commitments, beliefs, and decisions. Thus, if you can get your counterpart to agree with you on smaller issues at the start of the negotiation process, they are much more likely to agree with you on larger matters later on, in the interest of being consistent with their initial commitments.

8.2. Understanding Power in Negotition

Power, on the other hand, functions more directly than influence. It is the capability to control resources, make unilateral decisions, and enforce outcomes irrespective of resistance. It's important to note that the perception of power can sometimes be a more decisive factor than actual power. If you're perceived to have more power than you do, that perception could shape the negotiations in your favor.

Power in negotiation can come from many sources. For instance, having an attractive alternative to the negotiated deal (also known as BATNA - Best Alternative To a Negotiated Agreement) can provide you with substantial power. Having more information, demonstrating competence, or controlling resources can also yield significant power in negotiations.

Strategic use of power must be done with caution though. While power can give you the upper hand, it's important not to come across as overly aggressive or uncompromising, as it can damage relationships and trigger resistance from others. Striking a balance between the exertion of power and the maintenance of positive relations is a skill that all skilled negotiators must hone.

8.3. Leverage: The Balancing Act

Leverage in negotiation refers to the advantage that puts one party in a more favorable position to achieve their objectives. Leverage works by shifting the balance of a negotiation, favoring the party with the greater leverage. This might come from the unique value one party offers, having less to lose from walking away or deriving from the urgency or neediness of the other party.

Leverage operates differently from influence and power. While the former rely on the personal dynamics of the negotiators and their relationship, leverage is more situational and transactional. Therefore, effective utilization of leverage relies mainly on the ability to understand and maneuver within the specific context of each negotiation.

For example, superior market knowledge can offer significant leverage. If you know more about the market trends, competitor performance, and customer preferences than your counterpart, you can better leverage this information to your advantage. Similarly, having a strong network of connections can provide good leverage, as doing so can offer potential alternatives and validate your standing.

8.4. Achieving Balance between Influence, Power, and Leverage

The last piece of the puzzle in maximizing your advantage in negotiation involves the delicate act of balancing influence, power, and leverage. While each has its unique significance, employing them in a harmonious combination can result in a highly effective negotiation strategy.

Strike a balance by understanding when to use which approach. For instance, in the early stages of negotiation, you might rely more on influence to build rapport and lay a foundation of trust and understanding. As discussions become more substantive, you may lean on your power to move things forward and shape outcomes. Throughout, your leverage acts as the balance that can help swing the negotiation in your favor without tipping scales too drastically.

In conclusion, mastering the utilization of influence, power, and leverage equips you to be a persuasive negotiator. It enables you to tactfully navigate the negotiation process, adjust your strategy in response to unfolding events, and ultimately emerge with successful outcomes more often than not. By incorporating these techniques and strategies into your negotiation approach, you'll be better positioned to steer the negotiation process towards your ultimate goal.

Chapter 9. Negotiating in Difficult Situations

The journey through the multifarious terrain of negotiation often leads us to challenging situations. These trying times test not only the resources at our disposal, but they also evaluate our mental aptitude and agility, willpower, and ingenuity. Close your eyes and picture yourself facing a seemingly impossible negotiation scenario, such as dealing with a gregarious yet obstinate adversary, or an unpredictable, volatile negotiation scenario filled with aggression and rapidly changing terms. How do you emerge from such tough situations with a mutual agreement? As we navigate this chapter, we envelop ourselves in the exploration of these thorny territories, consequently empowering ourselves with tactics that thrive in the face of adversity.

9.1. The Blocking Stones: Identifying Difficult Scenarios

At the heart of negotiating in difficult situations lies the necessity to understand what these tricky scenarios entail. These situations are usually characterized by extreme emotions, high stakes, or aggressive, unyielding negotiation counterparts. Others may feature unclear objectives, mistrust between parties, or the presence of an enigmatic variable, invariably toppling the equation of negotiation. Knowing how to identify such scenarios is the stepping-stone that can then enable us to strategize our moves meticulously.

9.2. Navigating Emotional Rapids: Dealing with High Emotions

When negotiations take an emotional turn, the trajectory becomes much less predictable and much more turbulent. How does one steer clear of the emotional rapids to stay focused on the intended negotiation path? Here, the key is to maintain a calm demeanor, which can not only help to diffuse the situation but also anchor the negotiation in a more rational and constructive space. Active listening plays a pivotal role, helping us understand what fuels these emotions and how we might assuage them.

9.3. The Art of Taming the Storm: Dealing with Aggressive Counterparts

Being confronted with an aggressive counterpart can destabilize even the most experienced negotiator. Aggression can derail the process of constructive conversation, impacting the balance of the negotiation set-up. However, the master negotiator sees this as an opportunity, not a setback. Respond to aggression not with aggression, but with patience and understated assertiveness, showcasing your unshakeable commitment to finding a mutually beneficial outcome. It helps to reiterate shared goals and keep the conversation focused on the business at hand, rather than letting it descend into a personal battlefield.

9.4. Stepping into the Fog: Navigating Unclear Objectives and Miscommunication

Miscommunication and ambiguous objectives cloud the way and sow seeds of confusion and frustration between parties. In such a scenario, work towards clarity. Use candid dialogue and accurate articulation to dispel misunderstandings. Ensure both parties are on the same page about expectations, timelines, and responsibilities, coaxing out the obscured objectives into the bright light of understanding.

9.5. The High Ropes: Handling High-Stakes Negotiations

High-stakes negotiations are lined with substantial risk and potential reward. The pressure can be overwhelming, mental strain omnipresent. However, remember that it's the one who can steady their nerves while walking on these high ropes who triumphs. Preparation is an essential coping mechanism here: you can counterbalance anxiety by arming yourself with knowledge, planning for different outcomes, and setting realistic expectations.

9.6. The Maze: Overcoming Mistrust

Mistrust transforms negotiation into a maze of suspicion and doubt, inhibiting progress substantially. The negotiator's job, in this case, is to lay a trail of trustworthiness, fostering reliability with transparency, consistency, and dependable actions. Building bridges where mistrust has burned them is an art, requiring time, patience, and conscious effort.

9.7. Seizing Control: Encountering and Responding to the Unexpected

Despite careful planning and preparation, unforeseen elements can crop up, throwing a wrench in the works. How does one navigate these unexpected turns? The key here lies in flexibility and adaptability. Remember, every seeming roadblock can turn into an opportunity with the right perspective.

In the vast landscape of negotiation, formidable scenarios are as certain as the sun's rise. But a shrewd negotiator, equipped with the right strategies and the resilience to adapt, can transmute any situation into a growth-enabling challenge, a conduit to obtaining the sought results. The understanding of dealing with difficult circumstances is, therefore, an essential arsenal in your repertoire as you march towards becoming a master negotiator. This journey is certainly demanding, but the triumph at the end, always worthwhile.

Chapter 10. Strategic Concession-Making: The Give and Take of Negotiation

The act of negotiations, by its very nature, is seldom a straightforward path to a common agreement. It demands a melange of strategies, assertiveness, empathy, and a conceptual weapon seldom discussed in depth – the art of effective concession-making.

10.1. Understanding Concession-Making

In negotiation, "concession" refers to a negotiator giving up or agreeing to give up something. This may include tangible assets such as money, commodities, or time, but it can also involve more abstract elements like power dynamics, convenience or comfort zones. The act of making concessions is an integral part of the negotiation process— it demonstrates a willingness to compromise and paves the path towards mutual agreement.

Balancing the act of conceding appropriately can often be the cornerstone of a successful negotiation. Concede too much, and you risk being viewed as weak or even worse, leaving tangible or intangible value on the table, untreated and unused. Conversely, concede too little, and you may be perceived as inflexible or uncooperative, ultimately stalling the negotiation or even leading to disputes.

Designing an effective concession-making strategy requires an intricate understanding of the situation, the people involved, the stakes at hand, and how best to employ various negotiating techniques to craft acceptable concessions that can lead to a mutually beneficial outcome.

10.2. The Importance Of Structuring Concessions

Structuring your concessions is pivotal in negotiating. The process isn't just about deciding what to concede but involves a careful analysis of when, how, and in what sequence these moves should be made.

Timing: The timing of concessions can significantly impact the direction and outcome of the negotiation. Experience and research indicate that front-loading your concessions—making more significant concessions early on—can rapidly build trust and goodwill, fostering a more collaborative atmosphere. However, this should be done judiciously to avoid setting an expectation for more substantial concessions later. On the other hand, making significant concessions late in the negotiation process might signal desperation, ultimately undermining your perceived power or value in the negotiation.

Reciprocity: Ideally, every concession you make should invite a reciprocal concession from your counterpart. This principle of reciprocity is a powerful social norm that can be leveraged in negotiations. By making the first move, you can set a mutualistic tone for the negotiation where each party gives something up to generate common ground.

Sequence: The sequence of concessions, i.e., the order in which you make them, must also be thoughtfully planned. A common strategy is to start with smaller, less crucial concessions to build momentum and reciprocity, segueing into the big-ticket items.

10.3. The Strategy of Planned and Limited Concessions

A critical aspect of concessions lies in the "planning" and "limiting" nature of them. As a negotiator, you should come into the negotiation with a well-defined strategy regarding what, when, and how much you're prepared to concede. This concept extends to being purposely stingy in your concessions.

Limiting concessions is about establishing a level of assertiveness in your negotiating. Smaller, measured concessions demonstrate that you are engaged and receptive to compromising, but each concession is a deliberate choice, not a surrender to pressure.

Planning your concessions allows you to bring method to what might appear to outsiders as negotiation madness. Preparing before a negotiation provides an adept negotiator with the foresight to know when to hold firm, when to concede, and when to turn the tables by requesting a concession.

10.4. Concessions as a Signalling Tool

Concessions aren't purely about giving up something within a negotiation; they're also powerful tools for conveying information and influencing the perception of others. For instance, a carefully placed concession can signal the value you place on an issue or your willingness and ability to compromise. It can also be used to highlight the strength of your alternatives, test your negotiating partner's flexibility, or even draw attention away from other, more essential issues.

10.5. In Conclusion

In the crucible of negotiation, mastering the art of strategic concession-making can mean the difference between walking away feeling like a victor or a victim. By understanding and employing the concepts of structuring, planning, limiting, and signaling concessions, you can significantly enhance your negotiating prowess — transforming concession-making from a perceived act of surrender to an empowering tool in your negotiation arsenal.

Remember, negotiation is less about 'winning' in the traditional sense and more about finding a solution that both parties can live with. Concessions, when made correctly, bring you one step closer to that mutual middle ground, enabling you to influence outcomes, strengthen your bargaining position, and ultimately, achieve success in your negotiation journey.

Chapter 11. Maintaining Relationships Post-Negotiation: A Long-Term Perspective

In the dynamic realm of negotiation, it's often a misconception that the conclusion of a deal signifies the end of the negotiators' relationship. However, savvy negotiators understand that the end of a negotiation is merely the beginning of a new phase. This chapter is dedicated to providing a detailed guide on effectively maintaining relationships post-negotiation from a long-term perspective, which lays the foundation for future deals and partnerships.

11.1. The Importance of Post-Negotiation Relationships

While the negotiation process itself is crucial, maintaining relationships post-negotiation has equal - if not more - significance. Having a strong, positive relationship with your negotiation partner is vital as it facilitates future cooperation, builds trust, fosters mutual respect, and enables easier conflict resolution in the long run. It's important to note that post-negotiation is not just about maintaining contact, but it is about nurturing the relationship to foster longevity and mutual gain.

11.2. Ensuring Smooth Transition into Implementation

Upon reaching an agreement, one of the consequential steps is its successful implementation. This requires an ongoing relationship between the negotiating parties. To steer the transition smoothly, assemblage of a joint implementation team, composed of representatives from both parties, is often beneficial. Reiterate the details of the agreement in a shared meeting to ensure everyone is on the same page. Open, consistent, and timely communication is fundamental during this phase to prevent misunderstandings and discrepancies that might lead to conflicts.

11.3. Actively Seeking Feedback

Active solicitation of feedback is a paramount aspect of post-negotiation relationship maintenance. Feedback enables a clear understanding of the other party's level of satisfaction with the deal's outcome and the negotiation process. Likewise, respectfully sharing your own views on how the negotiation transpired can help improve future dealings. Regularly scheduled feedback sessions can provide valuable insights into areas of further refinement and potential opportunities for future collaboration.

11.4. Negotiating with a Perspective for Future Deals

The negotiations you encounter seldom happen in isolation. Most often, the relationships established with negotiation partners extend into the future, encapsulating innumerable negotiations over an extended period. To maintain this relationship, be proactive by demonstrating your commitment to the shared goals and success of your partner. Negotiate with a long-term perspective, considering the mutual benefits in future deals. This mindset promotes trust and loyalty, providing substantial advantages in future negotiations.

11.5. Dealing with Regret or Dissatisfaction

Not all negotiations result in outright satisfaction for both parties. There might arise instances of regret due to less favorable outcomes than expected. These feelings, if not appropriately managed, can strain the post-negotiation relationship. Emphasize on open dialogue and display empathy towards the other party's sentiments. Reflect on the negotiation process and explore the learnings together. Let the past negotiation serve as a lesson rather than a feud, thereby transforming it into a stepping stone towards improved future engagements.

11.6. Celebrating and Reflecting on the Success

Celebrating the mutual accomplishment post-negotiation acts as a positive reinforcement for the maintained relationship. Such celebrations acknowledge the efforts expended by both parties and commend the success achieved together. Coupling this with a reflective process enables both parties to gather learnings from the negotiation. This serves as a powerful tool for enhancing future interactions and creating a cycle of continuous improvement.

To sum up, the journey of negotiation transcends beyond the boardrooms and extends into the realm of relationships. The art of maintaining relationships post-negotiation demands a thoughtful long-term perspective, which in essence, includes values of respect, trust, and mutual benefit. By adopting the practices detailed in this chapter, professionals can enter into a sustained cycle of successful negotiations, nurturing profitable relationships in the process. This approach not only revolutionizes the outcomes of individual interactions, but also progressively elevates the entire narrative of negotiation.

www.ingramcontent.com/pod-product-compliance
Lightning Source LLC
Chambersburg PA
CBHW070141230526
45472CB00004B/1626